3 Day Guide to Tokyo

A 72-hour definitive guide on what to see, eat and enjoy in Tokyo, Japan

3 DAY CITY GUIDES

Image use under CC-BY License via Flickr

Cover Photo Credits:
Old Drug Store. Photo by Guwashi999
Hachiko. Photo by David Offf
Spring! Spring! Spring! Photo by Takashi .M
Shibuya Scramble Crossing. Photo by
Yoshikazu TAKADA

ISBN: 1508769192
ISBN-13: 978-1508769194

"We travel, initially, to lose ourselves; and we travel, next to find ourselves. We travel to open our hearts and eyes and learn more about the world than our newspapers will accommodate. We travel to bring what little we can, in our ignorance and knowledge, to those parts of the globe whose riches are differently dispersed. And we travel, in essence, to become young fools again- to slow time down and get taken in, and fall in love once more."
— Pico Iyer

CONTENTS

1 INTRODUCTION TO TOKYO

Shibuya Scramble Crossing. Photo by Yoshikazu TAKADA

Get ready to step into a world that is a heady blend of the old and the new. Tokyo is both modern and traditional, from its neon signs to its Shinto shrines. The sheer size of this city can give you a visual overload, from a visit to its 634m-high (2,080 ft.) SkyTree, the world's second tallest structure after Dubai's Burj Khalifa, to a trip to the stunning Studio Ghibli where you can see the classic characters from the films of Hayao Miyazaki. Tokyo is simply incomparable, with countless sights and historic pride, teeming with a population of approximately 12.5 million people residing in 2,100 sq. km (811 sq. miles) comprising almost one-fourth of Japan's population.

With structures built on top of each other, shaped like a jigsaw puzzle to maximize the existing plots of land, you will quickly understand that land is more precious than gold here. Japan's capital is a compressed concrete jungle, with a few parks and trees in between to break the monotony.

And yet, despite the limited space, Tokyo remains to be one of the safest cities in the world. The people here are very helpful, which is why it is said that the Japanese are their country's greatest assets.

Located in the heart of the country's largest island of Honshu, Tokyo pulsates a sense of dynamism with impressive skylines and an ever-present surge of people on the subway, train stations, its streets, and sidewalks. It is one of the most densely-populated cities in the world where space is very expensive so do not be surprised to find your hotel room to be compact and small. Despite this, Tokyo remains an elegant and fascinating city.

Here, things can get surreal as you can catch a glimpse or of amazing displays executed painstakingly close to reality. Live advertisements on its walls are just a part of

Japan's quirky and very creative approach to life. Their age-old habit of attention to detail is showcased not just through their ultra-modern structures, but also in their traditional cultural practices, from shows like *Kabuki* to their *Harajuku* fashion, all serving as proof of how the Japanese can push beyond the set boundaries.

As one of the world's leading giants in technology and scientific research, highly advanced innovations here are not only confined to electronic stores where you can find an impressive array of technological wonders, it even pours into the streets. A city that is always in a "rush", business here informally starts as early as seven o'clock in the morning and usually ends around eleven o'clock in the evening, even though official business hours are set from nine o'clock in the morning up to six o'clock in the evening.

Meals and lunches are taken more often than not in hurried batches, therefore you can find vending machines scattered all over the metropolis, for just about anything. Take for example, compact "power meals", catering to those who do not have the luxury of time to enjoy their lunch or dinner. It's an "on-the-go" kind of thing to maximize their daily activities.

Discipline is an attitude deeply-entrenched in the Japanese society, often times self-imposed, for they are always striving for excellence in all that they do. It has always been made clear right from childhood that precision, resilience and hard work will always lead to proficiency and success. One notable trait also of this Oriental culture is the importance that they place on achieving group objectives rather than individual goals, thus, it is common for them to achieve a consensus or agreement before they decide on anything.

Tokyo is comprised of small towns and neighborhoods clustered together, each with its own history, flavor and atmosphere. To get to know Tokyo's real charm and historical past, you need to dig deeper into the inner recesses of the city, past the present façade, into the narrow residential streets, lined with ma-and-pa shops, fruit stands and stores. There's the neighborhood *tofu* factory, the lunchbox stand, the grocery shop, and the tiny police station, where the cops know the residents by name and patrol the area on bikes. Carefully pruned bonsai trees line up the streets and sidewalks, framing wooden houses on narrow streets. Walk in the old downtown neighborhoods of *Asakusa* or *Yanaka* where you will be worlds apart from the trendy *Harajuku* or the high-rise *Shinju-ku*.

On the surface, Tokyo appears to be a gigantic metropolis where you may feel overwhelmed with its complexities. But once you get to know what is in its core, you will fall in love with its innate simplicity.

History

One of the 47 prefectures (a district under the government of a prefect - a chief officer, magistrate or regional governor in some countries) of Japan, Tokyo is the capital and is the seat of the Emperor of Japan and the Japanese government. Under Japanese law, Tokyo is designated as a metropolis although its administrative structure is similar to that of the other prefectures. Tokyo has 23 special wards, districts, towns, villages, a quasi-national park, and a national park. The wards are now separate, self-governing municipalities, each having their own mayor, a council, and the status of a city. Tokyo is in the Kanto region, a geographical area of Honshu (literally "Main Island"), and the largest island of Japan. It has seven prefectures namely Gunma, Tochigi, Ibaraki, Saitama, Tokyo, Chiba and Kanagawa.

In the early 12th century, Tokyo was a small fishing village named Edo, fortified by the Edo clan. Edo means estuary and it has been the seat of government since 1603. The Edo period was a time of samurai, tea ceremonies and calligraphy. When the shogunate fell in 1867, Emperor Meiji seized the reins of power and moved to Edo. Later on, Emperor Meiji renamed the place as Tokyo ("to" means "east" and "kyo" means "capital", after he moved his seat to the city from the old capital of Kyoto in 1868. He then established Tokyo as Japan's capital, and doors were thrown open on the country's borders and actively welcomed outside (particularly western) influences. He made Shinto the state religion. This period became known as the Meiji Revolution and it thrust Tokyo headlong into the 20th century. People flocked into the city from the countryside, educational standards were improving and arts and the theatre were blooming. But, in 1923, the city was devastated by the Great Kanto Earthquake, leaving 100,000 dead and nearly 2 million left homeless.

The effects of World War II on Tokyo has been vast and widespread, as air raids and bombings killed scores of people. The bombing of Tokyo in 1944 killed 75,000 and another one in 1945, left 200,000 people dead, with half of the entire city destroyed. Between 1943 and 1945, the effects of war resulted in countless deaths and widespread damage to properties. By the end of 1945, Tokyo's population dwindled from 6,700,000 to less than 2,800,000.

After the war, the people of Tokyo vowed to rebuild their lives and they did so. The 1970's brought new high-rise developments such as Sunshine 60, a new airport at Narita. Soon, the population increased to 11 million. Tokyo's subway and commuter rail network became one of the busiest in the world as more people moved to the area. In the 1980's, real estate prices soared high in what they call a real estate and debt bubble which burst in 1990s, leaving many companies, banks and individuals deeply in debt. A major recession followed making the 1990s Japan's lost decade.

Tokyo still sees new urban developments on large lots of less profitable land. Recent projects include Ebisu Garden Place, Tennozu Isle, Shiodome, Roppongi Hills, Shinagawa (now also a Shinkansen station), and the Marunouchi side of Tokyo Station. Land reclamation projects in Tokyo have continued for centuries, with the most prominent being the Odaiba area, now a major shopping and entertainment center.

21st century Tokyo is another amazing story as the country rises from the effects of another catastrophe. The 2011 Tohoku earthquake and tsunami devastated much of the northeastern coast of Honshu and was also felt in Tokyo. But due to the city's earthquake-resistant infrastructures, damage was minimal compared to those areas directly affected by the tsunami. The subsequent nuclear crisis caused by the tsunami has also left Tokyo unaffected, despite occasional spikes in radiation levels.

Tokyo was also selected to host the 2020 Summer Olympics and with this, it will be the first Asian city to host the prestigious games twice.

Today, Tokyo has the largest metropolitan economy in the world where 51 companies listed in the Global 500 are currently based in this city. It is also a major international finance center, housing the headquarters of the world's largest banks, insurance and financial companies and Tokyo serves as a hub for Japan's transportation, publishing, electronics and broadcasting industries. This city is one of the most expensive cities in the world and has been described as one of the three "command centers" for the world economy, along with New York and London.

Climate

Tokyo is just one of the few Asian countries that has a humid subtropical climate and four distinct seasons. It also has generally warm and moderate climate all-year round except during winter and during times of typhoons. You can also expect rainfall even during the driest months.

Spring

Spring in Japan lasts from March to May. The temperature can be cooler with occasional rain showers. Average temperatures range from 2°C to 17°C (35°F to 62°F). Spring is Tokyo's renowned season of colorful flowers. Scattered throughout the city are beautiful sites where you can enjoy these blooms, the most popular being the iconic Cherry Blossoms, which can be seen during the months of March and April.

Summer

Summer starts in June and lasts until August, and considered to be the hottest time of the year in the city. August is said to be the warmest with a temperature that can reach up to a high of 81°F (27°C). This is also the season of high humidity.

Autumn

Autumn begins in September and lasts through November, and is generally cooler with less humidity. During September however, there may still be days when temperatures can reach above 30°C. Fall or autumn is usually a welcome relief with clear blue skies and beautiful flowers.

Winter

The cold days of winter are characterized by chilly, gray days. Winter spans from December to February with the coldest month being January, averaging 42°F (6°C). Snowfall is common in the city during January and February, though temperatures rarely fall below freezing. Days are short with the sunset taking place around 5:00pm.

Typhoons

Tokyo has two rainy seasons. The first is June and the beginning of July. The other one is during the month of September. These are the least sunny months of the year. During the rainy season, Tokyo is particularly during the month of September, it is oftentimes visited by typhoon. Since the city is on the ocean side of the island, it is more susceptible to this type of weather disturbance. The most recent major typhoon in Japan happened in 1991, called Mireille, it was a category 4 typhoon which caused $560 billion in damage. Tokyo is also prone to be hit by tornados because the sea surface temperatures are not warm enough to sustain a powerful storm.

Best Time to Visit

Spring and autumn are the seasons where you can enjoy Tokyo at its best. These are months with generally cooler and more comfortable weather. These are the seasons when you can see the gorgeous splendor of the city's beautiful flowers in full bloom.

Language

Japanese is the sixth most spoken language in the world, with over 99% of the population using it. This language though, is rarely spoken outside of Japan. There are many theories as to where it originated but is very similar to Altaic languages (Turkish or Mongolian). It is recognized and acknowledged to be close in syntax to the Korean language. Standard Japanese is the language used in Tokyo.

Old Drug Store. Photo by Guwashi999

One of the biggest challenge of any foreigner in Tokyo is the language barrier. Most of the Japanese people do not speak nor write the English language. It will be like being transported into a totally unknown world speaking in a different tongue, in an unfamiliar way. Even signs, menus, and shop names are often in Japanese.

Japan's National Tourism Organization (JNTO), in an effort to help ease out the communication gap, created a nifty booklet called The Tourist's Language Handbook, with English translations of Japanese common words and phrases for everyday activities, from asking for directions, to shopping, to ordering foods, to staying in a Japanese inn. You can call the Tourist Information Center at telephone number 03/3201-3331 for assistance.

If you need to ask for directions, your best bet will to ask the younger people and the businessmen. They were taught English in school and can speak some English. You may also ask the people in the hotel to write down your desired destination in Japanese. You can just then show that piece of paper to taxi drivers or passers-by. If you get lost, look out for one of the police boxes called *koban*, which are virtually scattered all over the city. They have maps of their district and can pinpoint exactly where you want to go if you have the address with you.

Please bear in mind that the Japanese oral and written language are not exactly the same. The written language has three different types, Hiragana, Katakana and the most common one, Kanji. To be able to pronounce their words correctly, it will be advisable to ask help from a Japanese on how to pronounce an English word in the Japanese way.

Social Customs

Japanese is a race of rich legacy and cultural heritage and they are very proud of this. It pays to get to know the important aspects of this legacy before stepping into their land. To start off, all non-Japanese are called "*Gaijin*" literally translated as an "outside person". While this term is not generally meant to downgrade foreigners, it is fairly advisable to get to know some of the Japanese customs and traditions. You have to remember that aside from the language barrier, the Japanese exist in a homogenous society which is definitely complex and diverse in terms of socio-economic factors. Understanding their culture will provide you with a deeper insight on their norms and lifestyle.

Greetings

The most common form of greeting in Japan cannot be done through a smile nor a handshake. Upon meeting each other, whether for personal or business reason, they bow to each other. They do this gesture several times although, the more cosmopolitan ones may shake hands. Often, people will bow and shake hands simultaneously. They even have different ways of how they bow to greet people according age, status in society, gender and other categories. The lower the bow is, the greater the respect that is being paid to the other person.

Use of Names

Instead of addressing each other by first name, most Japanese use the family names followed by "*san*" (Mr./Miss/Mrs.), "*sensei*" (teacher but it is also used in addressing other professionals like dentists, physicians, politicians), or the title of the person being addressed. Since western names may be too hard for the Japanese to pronounce, nicknames are more appropriate. Japanese may address you by your first name or by your nickname.

Invitations

Invitations are extended either in person, by telephone or on printed invitations for formal receptions or dinners and all should be taken seriously. If invited to a meal, it is likely that it will be at a restaurant rather than at someone's home. It is polite to arrive on time, to take a small token of your appreciation (a potted plant, flowers, sweets), especially if you are going to a private home, and to say thank you afterwards by telephone, postcard, or letter.

Helpful Tips

Never leave your chopsticks upright in rice, since it is associated with the rice bowl placed in the funeral altar.

If you are visiting a sick person at home or in the hospital, never bring potted plants or flowers that change colors frequently, since this is associated with prolonging the sickness and the latter, making the sickness worst.

The numbers "4" and "9" are to be avoided in a gift or at other times because "4" = shi, has the same sound as the word death (shi), and "9" = ku, the word of suffering (ku)

No tipping is necessary here and they are usually not expecting any. Bumping someone on the street is a common occurrence, without them saying "excuse me".

Getting In

As one of the world's most progressive cities, Tokyo has two airports which handles majority of international flights and a number of domestic flights. Narita Airport which is located 60 kilometers outside of central Tokyo is the city's major air landing field. Hameda Airport, on the other hand is more centrally located and handles a smaller number of international flights and the majority of domestic flights.

For more information, you may visit:

http://www.japan-guide.com/e/e2017.html

Getting Around

Traditional Cart. Photo by Luke Ma

By train/subway

Exploring the sights of Tokyo can be done via their subway or the JR. Tokyo has a world-class, public transport system which can get you anywhere you want to go. It has the most sophisticated railway system in the world which traverses the entire city and its suburbs. The stations and stop points are conveniently located close enough to major sights and attractions in the metropolis. This is the most commonly used form of transportation in Tokyo and can be a more practical choice rather than taking a cab (which can be a bit pricey at times), plus it is a lot faster. Travel time will depend entirely on where you are heading as it may take some time to cover the distance especially if you need to do some transfers. In cases where you may need to change trains, expect it to consume a little more time due to the huge size of the stations where you have to walk.

The journey from Roppongi or Shibuya to Ueno, for example, takes approximately a half-hour because it's a straight shot on the subway, but a trip requiring transfers can take much longer. Traveling times to destinations along each line are posted on platform pillars, along with diagrams showing which train compartments are best for making quick transfers between lines.

Subways and trains are all very crowded and packed with commuters during the rush hours, usually in the morning between 8 to 9am.

Although, foreigners may find it more convenient as some of the stations have an English language ticket dispenser and some station stops are in English. Even inside the trains, there are signs and announcements in English. It will be very advisable to plan your journey and know which JR or subway line goes where and when. Once you already have a mapped out plan, then you can easily move from one station to another without much hassle.

All station exits are numbered and are yellow in color. The exits lead to major buildings, museums, and known addresses. If you get lost or got mixed up with any of these exits, you can just ask the person manning the ticket gates. Please take note that you always need to take the right exit points to save ample time (most stations have higher number of exit points like Shinjuku, which has more than 60 stations). When riding public transportation, it is also advisable to switch your mobile phones to mute or silent mode as a sign of good manner in Japanese culture.

Tickets

You can buy tickets at vending machines within all subway stations. Prices start at ¥160 for the minimum distance and will increase depending on how far your destination is. These vending machines give out change for whole bill payments and children are usually given discounted rates. To know the exact amount of your ticket fare, you may check out the posted lists on the subway map above the vending machines or the table listings.

There is also a list in the "Tourist Map of Tokyo", the guide issued by the Tourist Information Center. For easier and faster transactions, you may purchase a Suica or a

Pasmo card, an Integrated Circuit type of transportation charge card that you can purchase in the train stations. You simply swipe them on the sensor panels and go (no need to go through the long queues). Open tickets for one day use are also available (in several rates depending on how many places you need to see in a day) and can be used for multiple train and subway lines.

Prepaid tickets

You also have another option that can save you time and effort in paying for your fare. You can buy either a Suica or Pasmo card. There are also One-Day Open Tickets for unlimited 1-day rides on subways. The ¥710 1-day ticket (¥600 if you buy it at Narita Airport) is for use on Tokyo Metro lines (including the Ginza, Hibiya, Marunouchi, and Chiyoda lines), while the ¥1,000 1-day ticket can be used on all subway lines of both the Metro and Toei companies. These are sold at vending machines and are inserted into the ticket gate at the entrance to the platform, just like a regular ticket, except this time you'll retrieve it when you reach your destination.

If plan to travel on JR lines for more than a few days, consider buying a prepaid JR IO card, which can be found in most JR subway stations. IO cards come in denominations of ¥1000, ¥3000 and ¥5000 and can be purchased from some JR ticket machines. Insert the card into the automated turnstiles as you would a normal ticket, but don't forget to grab it as you exit the turnstile!

The turnstiles will automatically deduct the minimum fare as you enter the train system, and then any amount above that figure, if necessary, as you transfer and/or exit. If you have less than ¥160 left on the card, you will not be able to enter the subway system. Take the card to a ticket machine, then insert the card and whatever amount is necessary to bring the total on the card to ¥160. The machine will then spit out a new ticket and the now worthless JR IO card.

Much like the JR IO card, the Passnet card is a boon for anyone travelling the Tokyo subways. Passnet cards are sold by Tokyo Metro (SF Metro Card) or the Toei subway system (T-Card). These prepaid cards are valid for all the different subway lines and eliminate the need to buy several tickets for one journey. Purchase Passnet cards from ordinary automated ticket machines with a 'Passnet' logo (look for an orange-and-white running figure – presumably zipping through turnstiles). Cards are sold in denominations of ¥1000, ¥3000 and ¥5000. Insert the amount, push the Passnet button, then the cash amount button.

Or you can get a Tokyo Combination Ticket or Tokyo Free Kippu (Tokyo Round Tour Ticket), which costs about ¥1580 is a day pass that can be used on all JR, subway and bus lines within the Tokyo metropolitan area. It is available at most Green Window ticket counters, or at View Plaza (Travel Service Center), and at most Metro Subway Stations.

For more information, you may visit: http://www.japan-rail-pass.com/japan-by-rail/travel-tips/getting-around-in-tokyo

By Bus

Taking the bus instead of the subway or the trains can prove to be a bit of a challenge for tourists in Tokyo because of language barrier. The routes are most often than not listed and posted in Japanese and not in English, plus the drivers do not speak English (or speak very little of it!). Usual fare is around ¥200 (just drop it at the box at the front of the bus) and change is also available. They also accept Suica and Pasmo card. Major routes can be seen and used as a helpful guide in the Toei website: www.kotsu.metro.tokyo.jp. It can be very useful to take a snapshot of the routes you wish to take and show this to the driver or fellow passengers to get the exact directions on how to reach your destination.

If you are in a hurry, you can cover major sightseeing spots in the city by riding specific buses that go to known tourist spots. These buses follow a fixed route and offer fixed rates. One of them is the Toei's Tokyo Shitamachi Bus which departs from the Marunouchi north exit of Tokyo Station and stops at major points in the city. These buses travel in both directions at 30-minute intervals daily between 9am and 6:30pm. The fare is ¥200 each time you board (you can use a Suica card); or purchase a one-day Toei bus pass for ¥500.

By Boat

Tokyo can also be explored not only by land but also by water. This is a very unique experience as it gives a fresh take on the famous Tokyo skyline, silhouetted against the dramatic backdrop of the Sumida River.

The route is from Hinode Pier near Hamamatsucho and Hinode stations, and it cruises along the river to Asakusa. The trip takes approximately 40 minutes and costs ¥760. There's another boat that travels to Asakusa from Hama Rikyu Garden, while another route travels between Asakusa and Odaiba. For more information, you may get a brochure at the TIC or call the Tokyo Cruise Ship Co. at tel. 03/5733-4812. Schedules are also posted on its website at www.suijobus.co.jp.

Navigating around Tokyo may be challenging as negotiating routes can really become complicated (especially because of the language barrier). If in case that you get lost, as most tourists in Tokyo does, do not get frustrated as they say it is inevitable in this city where directions may somehow look like a maze.

For more information, you may visit: http://www.tokyometro.jp/en/ticket/search/index.php

Taxi

Rates of taxis in Tokyo are quite expensive. Fares start at ¥710 for the first 2km (1 1/4 miles) and increase ¥90 for each additional 288m (950 ft) or 40 seconds of waiting time. There are also smaller, more compact taxis for a maximum of four persons that charge slightly less, but they are fewer in number. Fares are posted on the back of the front passenger seat. Note that from 10pm to 5am, an extra 30% is added to your fare. Perhaps as an admission of how expensive taxis are, fares can also be paid by all major credit cards (though some companies require a minimum fare of ¥5,000).

With the exception of some major thoroughfares in the downtown area, you can hail a taxi from any street or go to a taxi stand or a major hotel. A red light above the dashboard shows if a taxi is free to pick up a passenger; a yellow light indicates that the taxi is occupied. Be sure to stand clear of the back left door -- it swings open automatically. Likewise, it shuts automatically once you're in. Taxi drivers are quite perturbed if you try to maneuver the door yourself. The law requires that back-seat passengers wear seat belts. Always make sure that you have your destination written out in Japanese since most taxi drivers don't speak English. There are so many taxis cruising Tokyo that you can hail one easily on most thoroughfares -- except when you need it most: when it's raining, or just after 1am on weekends, after all subways and trains have stopped. To call a major taxi company for a pickup, try Nihon Kotsu (tel. 03/5755-2336) for an English-speaking operator, or Kokusai (tel. 03/3505-6001; Japanese only). Note, however, that you'll be required to pay extra (usually not more than ¥400) for an immediate pickup.

Original Means of Transportation

Have you ever ridden a rickshaw? This is called "jinrikisha" in Japan. This is also one of the famous attractions in Tokyo which can remind you of the Edo days. The most famous neighborhood where you can catch a ride is Asakusa, but you can also ride one in Yanaka with Otowaya.

2 TOKYO DAY ONE

Tokyo will give you more things to do and plenty of sights to see in just 3 days. However with the right planning, you can still get the best out of this exciting city.

Let's start off with having breakfast at Cafe and Meal Muji in Ginza, Tokyo. Any trip to Tokyo should include a meal at this restaurant located at Muji. Food lovers will surely delight at the array of fresh breads, deli selections, salads, and more. Enjoy your meal in an impressively unpretentious restaurant with a unique natural feel. One trick for touring Tokyo will be to watch, observe and just go with the flow and this will start off with a visit to the very colorful district of Asakusa.

Address: Japan, 〒100-0006 Tokyo, Chiyoda, Yurakucho, 1-2-1, シアタークリエビル2階
Tel: +81 3-5501-1510

Asakusa District

Asakusa, Tokyo. Photo by Takayuki Miki

Have you ever seen a place pulsating with traditional colors mixed to the beat of modern, eclectic designs? Asakusa will give you just that.

Asakusa has a little bit of something for everyone. Do you want to know what the future has in store for you? You just need to donate 100 yen into the box near the Sensoji Temple and you will be able to know your Omikuji (pre-written strips of paper that can tell your future. All you need to do is to draw a stick that corresponds to your future. If you get a good future, keep it. If it is a bad future, tie it on the nearby pole, tree, or rack to make sure you that you will not bring the bad future with you. There are also traditional udon restaurants in this district and another treat are the Ningyoyaki (small Japanese cakes) vendors who create these delicious snacks in front of spectators. You can even order these freshly made goodies and afterwards enjoy a ride in a rickshaw, the traditional Japanese carriage from the Edo days. There are several other temples that you can visit in Asakusa and you can try exploring them if you have spare time.

In the 20th century, this district became the major entertainment hub in Tokyo famous for its theater, featuring Denkikan, the first dedicated movie in Japan.

Sensoji Temple

Senjoi Temple. Photo by Bob Owen

Asakusa is where you can find Senso-ji, a Buddhist Temple dedicated to Bodhisattva (a Buddhism belief as one of the four sublime states a human can achieve in life). Here, you will find a dragon themed fountain and a large pot emitting smoke which is believed to have purifying effects on the soul. Let the smoke waft towards you and observe what the people around you are doing. For the water, there is a proper procedure that needs to be followed. Grasp the ladle with your right hand, pour the water over your right hand and then do the same routine with your left hand. Then tilt the handle perpendicular and let the water run down the ladle to clean it, and then, put it back.

Additional Information:

Opening Hours: Daily 06:00am – 05:00pm

By Subway:

Tokyo Metro: Ginza Line – Asakusa Station
Toei Subway: Asakusa Line – Asakusa Station

Nakamise Shopping Arcade

Located just before Sensoji, after Kaminarimon or "Thunder Gate", Nakamise is one of the oldest shopping centers in Japan. Here, you will be greeted by the sights of massive paper lanterns dramatically painted in vivid red-and-black tones to suggest thunderclouds and lightning. This is a 250 meter street between Kaminarimon and Hozomon gates in Asakusa. It has around 90 shops that sell a wide variety of goods from snacks to souvenirs like yukata, keychains and folding fans (even luxury chopsticks!). This place can be very charming at night when it is less crowded.

Kaminarimon, Asakusa. Tokyo, Japan. Photo by OiMax

Additional Information:

Hours: Daily 10:00am – 5:00pm

By Subway:

Tokyo Metro: Ginza Line – Asakusa Station
Toei Subway: Asakusa Line – Asakusa Station

The SkyTree

See the second tallest structure in the world! Tokyo SkyTree has a full height of 634 meters (2,080 ft.) and is currently the world's highest stand –alone communication tower.

SkyTree. Photo by Fabian Reus

This soaring structure also serves as the centerpiece of a large commercial complex and it houses broadcasting networks, a restaurant and observation tower. The design showcases a fusion of neo-futuristic appeal combining it with the traditional beauty of Japan. The base is formed into a tripod and the tower's structure is cylindrical to provide a vantage point for the panoramic views of the city. The upper observatory deck features a spiral, glass-covered skywalk where you can ascend the last 5 meters to the highest point at the upper platform. This is truly an exciting experience! A section of the glass flooring will even allow you to take a peek at the downward view of the busy streets below.

There are several ways of purchasing a ticket to get into the Tokyo SkyTree Observation Deck:

You can buy your tickets online (only Japanese issued credit cards are accepted here)

Purchase day tickets at the "Tokyo SkyTree 4th floor ticket counter".

Use travel plans including admission tickets via your travel agents.

Some accommodation packages may include admission tickets. You may visit http://www.tokyo-skytree.jp/en/hotel/ for more information.

Ebisu

Drop by to see this local neighborhood serving as home to Japan Beer Brewery Facilities. Formerly known as the place where Yebisu Beer was made (named after Ebisu, one of the Japanese Seven Gods of Fortune), the drink was later renamed Sapporo Beer, after the brewery moved to Chiba in 1988. Today, the main attraction here is the Yebisu (pronounced without the "y") Garden Place. It has boutiques, vintage stores and patisseries all within walking distance from the Ebisu station. It is also home to many bars and restaurants, from izakaya-style restaurants, to English-style pubs, to old-fashioned stand and drink bars. A lot of locals frequent these places, and it's a great experience to rub elbows with them.

Ebisu. Photo by Takayuki Miki (三木貴幸)

Ginza

Have a glimpse of the snobbish Tokyo appeal in this pricey area where sophistication is the norm. A trip here need not be totally expensive though, as there are sights that you can explore without breaking the bank. If your game is to go shopping for the latest in the gadget arena, the Sony building and the Apple store can be your best bet. Both of them offer some of the trendiest products in the world. The Mitsukoshi Department store is another story, as it provides a different kind of shopping experience in one of Japan's first western style department stores dating back the 1800's.

There are other interesting places to visit here like the Kabuki-za Theatre, a beautiful structure of traditional design built from modern materials. Here, you can catch daily performances (tickets can bought at the door for under 1000 yen). The other must-see sights in Ginza are as follows:

Tsujiki Honganji

Set foot in a traditional Buddhist temple. Located in Ginza (by walking down Harumi Don Avenue, and the turning left into Shin Ohashi Avenue), you can find this beautiful temple. Built in 1671, it is an impressive architectural piece which was razed by the Great Fire of Tokyo in 1657, destroyed by earthquake in 1923, but was rebuilt in 1935. This is the head of the Jodo Shinshu denomination and is a very symbolic shrine for Buddhism.

Address: 3-15-1, Tsujiki, Chuo, Tokyo 104-8435

Phone: +81 3 3541 1131

Tsujiki Fish Market

Head back to Harumi Don and cross over to the vicinity of the largest fish wholesale market in Asia. Seafood is predominantly part of the Japanese diet and is part and parcel of their daily meal. Trading climaxes in the morning but you can catch a glimpse of the deserted streets in the afternoon as well, when the market takes on a quieter atmosphere.

Tsujiki Fish Market. Photo by James Trosh

Nakajin Capsule Apartment

At first glance, you will wonder about this building's main purpose and function. The design is odd and unique and it serves as a compact residential place. The Nakajin Capsule Apartment is the world's first attempt at a capsule or cube space, in which a person can live in a "micro space" (remember Tokyo is densely populated). Each capsule is approximately only three meters by five meters square. The bed takes up most of the space and all the appliances needed for everyday living surround it. There's also a convenience store at the first floor. In the recent years, this structure which was built in 1970 is now in the state of dilapidation. An icon of Tokyo's urban landscape, there has been an on-going debate for its preservation.

Address: Located in Ginza, a shopping area in the heart of Tokyo.

Odaiba

Literally meaning the "fort", Odaiba is a popular shopping and entertainment district on a manmade island in Tokyo Bay. It originated as a set of small man made islands built towards the end of the Edo period (1600-1868) to protect Tokyo from possible attacks from the sea.

Over the years, the smaller islands were joined together by massive landfills and it heralded the construction and development of a futuristic residential and business district which slowed down during the "bubble economy" in the early 1990's. The second half of 1990's saw Odaiba rising back despite the initial setbacks. Several hotels, shopping malls and the Yurikamonte elevated line opened offering a wide selection of shopping, dining and leisure options.

Roppongi

Figure 1Roppongi Hills Mori Tower. Photo by Stefan

Revel in city's most popular nightlife district with friendly bars, restaurants and night clubs. Roppongi is also the home of many foreign embassies and a large expat community. Changing the face of the district are two of Tokyo's recent developments, Roppongi Hills and Tokyo Midtown, featuring elegant retail, leisure and residential spaces, offices and luxury hotels. Roppongi Hills is dubbed as a city within a city with residential spaces, offices and recreational facilities all within one building complex.

Similarly, Tokyo Midtown is another amazing development that offers residential, commercial and entertainment facilities just like its counterpart. It also has a museum, the Suntory Museum of the Arts, as well as stylish shops and restaurants. Aside from the said museum, there are several more that can found in this district which include the National Art Center, reputedly Japan's largest art museum.

3 TOKYO DAY TWO

After a very tiring yet fulfilling first day in Tokyo, you certainly deserve a treat! Bills at Omotesando Harajuku, opened by Australian chef Bill Granger, a signature name carried by the "best breakfast in the world" resto in Sydney. It is one of the most popular breakfast places in Tokyo. Getting a place here is not easy so be ready to fall into queue. You may try their classics like the Ricotta Hotcakes, Fresh Banana & Honeycomb Butter and the Scrambled Organic Eggs with Toast. Or, you can have the Full Aussie Breakfast with Toast, Mushrooms, Bacon, Roast Tomato and Chipolatas.

After such a heart-filling treat, you can now head off to some more exciting places in Tokyo.

Address: Japan, 〒150-0001 東京都渋谷区 神宮前4-30-3 東急プラザ表参道原宿7F
Tel: +81 3-5772-1133

Shinjuku

Golden Street Shinjuku, Tokyo. Photo by Takashi .M

Set foot in the bustling Shinjuku district, the center of Tokyo's culture. The Tokyo Metropolitan Government building can be found here. Shopping areas dot the streets such as department stores and large-scale shops. There is actually an array of fashion buildings around the Southwest exit. You will also notice and admire a number of public art installations in the business area. JR Shinjuku Station is the busiest station in Tokyo serving about 3.5 million passengers each day. This is literally a place teeming with people and if you are already longing to have a respite, head towards the Shinjuku Gyoen National Garden, the largest and most popular park in Tokyo, located just a short walk from the Shinjuku station. It has spacious lawns, meandering walking paths and tranquil scenery which can give you some precious moments to relax in an oasis within a busy city.

Harajuku

Take a moment to imagine the place of trendy fashion in Tokyo. Between Shinjuku and Shibuya on Yamamote Line, is where you can find Japan's most extreme cultures and chic styles. The focal point here is Takeshita Dori (Taskehita Street) and its side streets which are lined with trendy shops, fashion boutiques, used clothes stores, crepe stands and fast food outlets, all symbolizing the lifestyle of today's young generation. To catch the best glimpse of the Harajuku story is to come here on a Sunday, where you can see a lot of young people gather around Harajuku station and engage in cosplay (costume play), dressed up in eccentric costumes to resemble anime characters, punk musicians and a lot more.

Omotesando, located just south of Takeshita Dori, is a broad tree lined avenue where you can find brand name and signature shops, cafes and restaurants. Harajuku though is not entirely about trends and fashion. **Meiji Jingu**, one of Tokyo's major shrine dedicated to the defied spirits of Emperor Meiji (a popular Emperor who reigned from 1867 to 1912), is also located here, as well as the Nezu Museum which has an impressive collection of various Asian art and a traditional Japanese garden.

Kanda

Get off the beaten track and go to Kanda. Not a prime tourist district, this place is more of a typical local residential area and is the location of many universities, making it Tokyo's academic center. Deep within Kanda are several interesting neighborhoods, such as the **Ochanomizu** musical instrument area, the **Jimbocho** book area and the famous electronic and anime mecca, **Akibahara.**

Kanda, Tokyo. Photo by Takashi .M

Akibahara

Be fascinated in the world of the new generation! Located in central Tokyo, this place is famous for its many electronic shops. Recently, it has gained recognition as the center of Japan's *otaku* (diehard fan) culture, and many shops and establishments devoted to anime and manga (comic series corresponding to a Japanese style which originated in the mid-1900's). This book gained popularity not just in Japan but all over the world, read by both genders and all ages. Dozens of stores sell video games, figurines, card games and other collectibles filled in between the electronic retailers. In addition to these shops, various other animation related establishments have become popular in the area, particularly maid cafes, internet cafes where customers can read comics and watch DVD's in addition to having access to the internet. This is definitely an otaku and anime heaven! On Sundays, Chuo Dori, the main street, is closed to traffic.

Jimbocho

This is the world of books! Jimbocho is the place where you can delve into practically anything published and bound, new and old, soft-bound and hard-bound manuscripts both in Japanese and English. This is the book and shopping mecca of Japan where you can hunt for the best bargains, rare collector's editions and even unusual books. It is also the home of publishing houses, literary agents, and the prestigious Literature Preservation Society and Tokyo Book Binding Club. This district attracts authors and intellectuals who spend hours reading or debating in the cafes. Numerous universities are also located in the area such as Meiji University, Hosei University, Toyo Gakuen University, to name a few.

Jimbocho is also known as one of Japan's largest sports shopping neighborhoods. There are around 50 sports shops in the area, specializing in snowboard and ski gear, many of these stores are extremely competitive with each other. This place is also the best spot if you want to try small cheap eateries that cater to the area's budget shoppers and students. Just expect to wait in line for an hour of enjoying a perfect bowl of ramen.

Ochanomizu

Tinker the keys of the musical instruments on sale at Ochanomizu. Strike a few chords and enjoy playing good music before deciding on which one to buy. Famous for its musical instrument stores, it is also a popular district for bargain-conscious musicians. *Ocha-no-mizu* means "tea water" after the nearby Kanda River from which water was extracted to make the shogun's tea during the Edo period.
This neighborhood in Tokyo extends from the Yushima section of Bonkyo-ku to the Kanda section of Chiyoda-ku. A lot of famous Japanese universities are in this area.

Wooden Votive Tablet at Yushima Tenman-gū Shrine, Yushima, Bunkyo-ku, Tokyo. Photo by Yoshikazu TAKADA

Onsen

Immerse yourself literally into a bath of hot spring waters. Nothing can be more relaxing that soaking yourself in a good, calming and relaxing dip, the Japanese way. You are in a country of the most active volcanoes in the world thus, it has an abundance of hot springs. Traditionally, Japanese of the Edo days had to trek to spa towns like Hakone and Atami if they wanted to enjoy bathing in hot spring waters but today's Tokyoites have newer and more accessible options. You can now find diverse range of onsen (hot baths) in Tokyo, where you can enjoy and relax a hot spring bath without leaving the city.

Hot spring bath at Kurokawa Onsen, Kyushu. Photo by David McKelvey

For more information, you may visit:
http://www.secret-japan.com/forum/onsen-in-and-around-tokyo-t312.html

4 TOKYO DAY THREE

Have a one-of-a kind breakfast experience at Cure Maid Cafe, in Akibahara. The first permanent maid cafe, established in 2001. These cafes are now so embedded in Japanese media and fetish culture and is increasingly gaining much popularity. Maid cafes are a subcategory of cosplay restaurants found predominantly in Japan where waitresses are dressed in maid costumes, and act as servants. They treat their customers as masters (and mistresses) in a private home, rather than cafe patrons. Cure Maid Cafe is just a short walk off of the main Chuo-dori and it is also close to the Suehirocho station. Food here is Japanese with a European flair. You can try their pork cutlets with spaghetti or rice and a variety of other light but hearty meals. They also have a wide selection of desserts like Earl grey chiffon cake and strawberry waffles. This can perfectly match with iced tea or orange juice.

Address: 3 Chome-15-5 Sotokanda, Chiyoda, Tokyo, Japan
Tel: +81 3-3258-3161

Ueno

Spring! Spring! Spring! Photo by Takashi .M

After a hearty breakfast, head off to Ueno Park in Central Tokyo. The park grounds were originally part of the Kaneji Temple, which used to be one of the city's largest and wealthiest temples and served as the temple of the Tokugawa clan during the Edo Period. See its many museums, especially the Tokyo National Museum, the oldest and largest museum in Japan. It is made up of many buildings, each like a separate museum in itself. Marvel at the largest collection of national treasures and important cultural items from Japan's distant past. This park is also one of the most popular spots to enjoy the famous cherry blossoms, with more than 1000 cherry trees lining its central pathway. The cherry blossoms are usually in full bloom during the month of March and April.

Hachiko

Hachiko. Photo by David Offf

See for yourself the very famous statue of Hachiko. Many people from all over the world must have heard of Hachiko, the loyal Akita dog who patiently and devotedly waited for his master every day, for 10 long years in front of the Shibuya Station for his master to return in 1925. His owner, Hidesaburo Ueno, was a professor at the University of Tokyo who died of cerebral hemorrhage and never came back. Hachiko didn't know of this and so he waited and waited until his own demise in 1935.

Today, Hachiko has a statue erected in his honor and a replica of the original still stands near Shibuya Station. Very recently, a new statue of the dog and the master reunited today stands at the University of Tokyo's agriculture department where Ueno served for over 20 years.

Kamakura

Kamakura, Kanagawa Japan. Photo by OiMax

On the third and last day of stay in Tokyo, it will be best to explore some day trips in a place less than an hour from Shibuya station by commuter train, in a coastal town in Kanagawa Prefecture, less than an hour south of Tokyo. Kamakura has two hiking trails and a beach, as it is on the Pacific coast. During the summer months, its beaches also attracts large crowds. This is also the political center of Japan with numerous temples, shrines and other historical monuments.

A unique tourist attraction, it will provide a cultural experience of discovery and learning, as well as a natural respite. Travel to this place and see for yourself the Daibutsu, a big bronze Buddha statue which was casted in 1252. It's grand stature climbs more than 13 meters, or 43 feet high, and is known to be the second largest in Japan. This Buddha statue symbolizes the predominant religion of the locals and has always been showcased in most Japanese iconic photographs. You can reach the site via the JR train. It is open daily from 7am to 6pm although they close early on winters).

Another interesting place to visit is Hase-dera, or the Hase Kannon Temple, also in the Kamakura. The temple stands in a location that calmly overlooks the sea. Inside the temple, you can find Kannon, the Japanese goddess of mercy, whose statue was created in the 18th century, out of camphor wood and stands at 30 feet high. The statue has 11 heads, with each head showing a different facial expression signifying the goddess' compassion for all kinds of suffering. Here you will also find Jizo statues, believed to be the guardian of the unborn, stillborn and aborted children. After exploring the temples and being bewitched by the gods and goddesses and their enchanting stories, take a moment relax and enjoy the lush gardens surrounding the temple that epitomize a typical Japanese landscaping design.

5 BEST PLACES (EAT, WINE & DINE)

TAN-TAN-MEN (O-okayama, Tokyo, Japan). Photo by t-mizo

A Japanese culinary adventure is a totally unique gastronomic treat that can tickle and satisfy your taste buds, long after your trip is over. The Japanese are very passionate about their food and the options here, can be endless.

Rokurinsha Tokyo (Ramen Street)

Slurping ramen in Japan means you are enjoying your food. So, go ahead and slurp them up in this restaurant which is located in level B1 of First Avenue Tokyo Station, serving the "best tsukemen in the city". It is a favorite of both the locals and tourists thus be prepared to wait in line especially during peak hours. This locale is casual, with quick service and budget-friendly costs.

Address: 1-9-1 Marunochi, Chiyoda, Tokyo
Tel: +81 3 3286 0166

Gogyo

Savor their Burnt Miso Ramen, which is also a local favorite. Bear in mind they close for break at 4:30pm. They are serving purely Japanese food which include, of course, ramen.

Address: 1-4-36 Nishiazabu, Minato
Tel: +81 3 5775 5566

Hachibe

The best sushi and sashimi in the city is served here. You can expect the finest quality food selection, guaranteed fresh served omakase or ala carte. They have a sake bar too. Cost is very affordable and service is impeccable.

Address: 1-7-6 Ebişu, Tokyo
Tel: +81 3 3280 8181

Tonkatsu Wako

This place is located inside Tokyo train station and is very famous for tonkatsu (breaded pork chop). They offer quick service in a very casual ambience.

Address: 6-5-1 Nishishinjuku, Shinjuku
Tel: +81 3 3348 0610

Ginza Akebono Mochi Shop

Craving for some sweets? Try munching on some mochi, the traditional Japanese sweets which comes in a variety of flavors. This is a local favorite and a lot of people frequent here. This is a to-go shop so there are no seats available.

Address: 5-7-19 Ginza Chuo, Tokyo
Tel: +81 3 3571 3640

Jangara Ramen

Kyushu ramen is the specialty here and how you want to have it is entirely up to you. At this bright and breezy noodle house, you can specify particular broths (light or heavy), type of noodles (thick or thin), quantities and toppings.

Address: 1-13-21 Jingu-mae, Shibuya-ku, Tokyo
Tel: +81 3 3404 5572

Nigiro Cafe

This cafe has already gained quite a following since it opened its doors. If you are looking for a place for brunch but would like to avoid the JPY5000 price tag of Roy's, this is the spot for you. Sit outside and enjoy heavenly eggs benedict while reading an English magazine placed on the rack for your enjoyment. It offers teatime treats during the afternoon hours and California-style dishes at night. Come with friends or alone, it is a great place to relax.

Address: R. Matsumura Building 1F
1-9-6 Musashino-shi, Minami-cho
Tel: +81 0 422 40 9533

6 TOKYO NIGHTLIFE

Night Life @ Shinjuku, Tokyo. Photo by Kevin Poh

Tokyo at night turns into one of the craziest cities in the world. Entertainment districts stay open until the wee hours of the morning. The city has all forms of fun and entertainment that you can imagine - from jazz, reggae, gay bars, dance Tokyo has no one center of nighttime activity. There are many nightspots spread throughout the city, each with its own atmosphere, price range, and clientele. Most famous are probably Ginza, Kabuki-cho in

Shinjuku, and Roppongi. Before heading out to a
night spot of your choice, be sure to walk around
the neighborhoods and absorb the atmosphere. The
streets will be crowded, the neon lights will be
overwhelming, and you'll never know what you
might discover on your own.

Traditional Entertainment

Kabuki Theater

Watch and enjoy a traditional and highly
stylized form of Japanese theatre. These are
visually and very beautiful performances in
which all the roles are played by men. At the
Kabuki-za Theatre in Ginza, performances
usually start late in the morning and take place
on most days.

Address: Ginza 4-12-15, Chuo-ku
Phone: +81 3 3545 6800

ageHa

The biggest club in Tokyo with three dance
floors, an outdoor swimming pool and
numerous chill-out areas and bars, take your
pick and groove to the blasting music. It

located at Shin-Kiba and can be reached by a free shuttle bus from Shibuya (Roppongi-dori Street) that comes every 30 minutes.

Address: 2-2-10, Shinkiba, koto-ku, Tokyo
Phone: +81 3 5534 2525

Womb

Located just a 15 minute walk away from Shibuya, the Womb offers a vast dance floor, great lighting and a superb sound system giving you the perfect recipe for a night of dancing and fun! A giant mirrored ball hangs from the center of the main dance floor, reflecting the multitude of lights into every corner of the hall. This establishment houses the best DJs in the city.

Address: 1F 2-16 Maruyamatyo, Shibuya-ku
Phone: +81 3 5459 0039

Genius

This is not a typical, casual party place, instead the air here is more formal and stylish. Genius is located in Ginza, the high end district of branded boutiques and chic restaurants. Guests are usually dressed up in suits, glittering dresses and accessories.

Address: 6-4-6 Ginza, Chuo-ku
Phone: +81 3 3571 5830

Feria

This place is another stylish night club occupying all 5 floors of the entire building in Roppongi. It is a popular spot for both Japanese and foreigners who are looking to have a night of fun. Its Ristorante offers delectable cuisines and the best wines and drinks. The bar at the rooftop offers a romantic night scenery of the city.

Address: 7-13-7 Roppongi minato-ku
Phone: +81 3 5785 0656

7 PLACES TO STAY (LUXURIOUS, MID-RANGE, BUDGET)

Mandarin Oriental Tokyo. Photo by Norio NAKAYAMA

Luxurious

The Peninsula Tokyo

Striving for an understated Zen-like simplicity, starting from its lobby which serves their signature afternoon tea accompanied by live classical music, the interiors are quite simple and void of embellishments. The rooms, beginning at 51 sq. m., are among the Tokyo's largest and offers a view of the Imperial Palace and Hibiya Park. They feature the latest in high-tech luxury, dressing rooms with vanity counters and dryers, valet boxes, and bathrooms with mood lighting and roomy enough for couples, even in the tub. Other perks include a great location near Marunouchi and Ginza, a Rolls Royce that will deliver you anywhere within a 2-km (approximately 1 mile) radius for free, complimentary iPods to guide you through the surrounding neighborhood, and the Peninsula Academy with a changing roster of classes and experiences that can include making washi (Japanese paper) or a tour of a sake brewery.

Address: 1-8-1 Yurakucho, Chiyoda-ku
Phone: +81 3 6270 2888

Imperial Hotel Tokyo

One of Tokyo's oldest hotels, with a prime location near subway stations, it first opened in 1890 at the request of the Imperial family.

Rooms are spread in the main building, popular with the Japanese because of showers located outside of tubs (which allows them to bathe in traditional fashion), and in a 31-story tower added in 1983, preferred by foreigners. Although access to the tower is a bit cumbersome, via a second-floor passageway, and rooms are smaller, foreign guests tend to like rooms here because views are better (with a choice of either the Ginza with its sparkling neon or Hibiya Park and Imperial Palace) and this is where the pool and gym are located.

Address: 1-1-1 Uchisaiwaicho, Chiyoda-ku
Phone: +81 3 3504 1111

Mandarin Oriental Tokyo

Located in the Nihonbashi Mitsui Tower, this is a world-class hotel which has executive suites which may lack space but runs high with ultimate comfort. The more expensive suites come with an open living room that showcases a commanding view of the city. It also has luxurious bathrooms where you can relax in the spacious bathtubs.

Address: 2-1-1 Nihonbashi Muromachi, Chuo-ku
Phone: +81 3 3270 8800

Mid-range

Conrad Tokyo

A contemporary hotel with creative features starting with the large sumi-e (Japanese brush painting) in the lobby by Toko Shinoda, just one of 23 leading Japanese craftsmen with artwork gracing the hotel. It also has one of the city's largest spa and fitness centers, occupying the entire 29th floor with 10 treatment rooms, including a couple's room with a hinoki (cypress) tub, a 25-meter pool and a gym. This hotel has fantastic views over Hama Riku Garden of Tokyo Bay and Odaiba. Rooms are large, starting at 48m (516 sq. ft.). The cheapest face the city, and the bayside rooms, which take full advantage of the panoramic views are great places to relax. All rooms have bathrooms designed for two people. There are several options for fine dining, but most impressive is China Blue for its contemporary Cantonese cuisine and sweeping views over the bay.

Located a short walk from the Ginza and Shiodome.

Address: Minato-ku, near Ginza, Tokyo
Phone: +81 3 388 8000

Hotel Wing International Meguro

This hotel is very functional, and is very ideal for business and pleasure. It has internet access in all guest rooms, a Breakfast Restaurant, and a number of facilities and amenities for its guests.

Address: 1-3-13, Meguro, Meguro-ku, Tokyo
Phone: +81 3 3779 6311

Budget

The b roppongi

The b roppongi, open since 2004, was the first of nine business hotels under the "b" brand. Its quirky name is based on four concepts: a comfortable bed, a good breakfast (which nonetheless costs extra), a balanced life, and a contemporary and relaxed atmosphere for conducting business. What this boils down to is a boutique business hotel that is more stylish than most of its genre, with beds that are indeed comfortable and have focused reading lamps. Otherwise, standard and superior rooms are your typical business-hotel tiny size, so travelers yearning for a bit more space might want to splurge on a deluxe, which offers the advantage of more windows in addition to more space. Facilities are practically nonexistent, unless you count the free coffee in the lobby, but in any case, Roppongi's nightlife is just outside the door. Other b hotels in Tokyo are in Ochanomizu, Akasaka, Ikebukuro, Sangenjaya, and Hachioji.

Address: 3 Chrome 9-8 Roppongi, Minato, Tokyo
Phone: +81 3 5412 0451

Hotel New Otani

The New Otani boasts one of the city's best hotel gardens, more than 400 years old and once the private estate of a feudal lord. Spreading over 4 hectares (10 acres), it contains ponds filled with koi, waterfalls, arched bridges, manicured bushes (the many azaleas are especially striking in spring), stone lanterns, bamboo groves, and a stone garden. The large outdoor pool, shrouded by greenery, provides more privacy than most hotel pools and is free for members of Otani Club International (membership is free). That's about it, however, when it comes to communing with nature, as this is one of Tokyo's largest hotels (be sure to pick up hotel and garden maps at the concierge, because you're going to need them). Its 31 restaurants and 6 bars draw huge crowds of locals, especially its very popular Garden Lounge offering the best views of the garden and The Sky revolving restaurant. Rooms are spread among the main building, built for the 1964 Olympics and offering the best up-close views of the garden, and the 40-story Garden Tower with views over the glittering city. Because rates are the same regardless of view, ask for a room facing the garden. Hotel facilities are so exhaustive this is like a city within a city; folks who shun crowds will be happier elsewhere.

Address: 4-1 Kioicho, Chiyoda, Tokyo
Phone: +81 3 3265 1111

Khaosan Tokyo Guest House Ninja

This is one of the cheapest place to stay in the city and is a popular spot for backpackers. It offers a communal space, dormitory-type of accommodation with free Wi-Fi and a large TV with cable. They cater to short-term as well as long-term guests. This guest house is ideal for budget travelers.

Address: 2-5-1 Nihombashi Bakurocho, Chuo-ku
Phone: +81 3 6905 9205

8 OTHER INTERESTING PLACES TO VISIT

A photographer capturing view from Mt Fuji. Photo by Azlan DuPree

Hakone

Part of Fuji-Hakone-Izu National Park, Hakone is one of the closest and most popular weekend destinations for residents of Tokyo. Beautiful Hakone has about everything a vacationer could wish for -- hot-spring resorts, mountains, lakes, breathtaking views of Mount Fuji, and interesting historical sites. You can tour Hakone as a day trip if you leave early in the morning and limit your sightseeing to a few key attractions, but adding an overnight stay -- complete with a soak in a hot-spring tub -- is much more rewarding. If you can, travel on a weekday, when modes of transportation are less crowded and some hotels offer cheaper weekday rates.

Nippara Cave

Explore the largest limestone cave in the Kanto region which is more than 800 meters deep, 280 meters of which is illuminated and can be explored. This vast underground space is an example of the inconceivable wonders of nature. Fascinating views on the inside will show you various formations of stalactites and stalagmites, which took almost 400 years to grow (from slow, steady trickling of water droplets). Near the cave are different rock formations of various heights and sizes.

Nippara Limestone Cave. Photo by Dick Thomas Johnson

Azabu Juban

Azabujuban is a beautiful residential area in the Minato district of central Tokyo with a perfect mix of quaint shops, upscale restaurants and trendy cafés. Its close proximity to Roppongi (it's literally right behind Roppongi Hills) and the many Embassies around the area make it one of the most popular and desirable residential areas in Tokyo. Many celebrities and politicians live in the neighborhood. The main street of Azabujuban is a stretch of adorable cobbled stone pavement that winds through the middle of the neighborhood, evoking a fun and friendly small town feeling, even though it is in the middle of bustling Tokyo.

Mt. Takao-san

This is the closest natural recreation areas to central Tokyo. It has a beautiful scenery, an interesting temple and attractive hiking opportunities. Although it is outside the city center, this mountain is still located within metropolitan Tokyo and takes only 50 minutes and 390 yen to reach from Shinjuku.

9 CONCLUSION

Morning Glow in Tokyo. Photo by Bernhard Friess

Describing Tokyo to someone who has never been there before is a formidable task. After all, how do you describe a huge metropolis that seems like part of another planet? Much of the anxiety associated with travel comes from a fear of the unknown, and not knowing what to expect can give even seasoned travelers, butterflies. But these are all part of the excitement that Tokyo can give, with all its relentless surprises.

Exploring Tokyo will be like a big challenge that one would love to conquer. This dynamic city can be very elusive, oftentimes extravagant and expensive, seductively beautiful yet very hard to understand. To grasp its full essence will never be easy, but its captivating charm will surely be felt at your core. At the end of the day, you will simply realize that it was all worth it. Tokyo is indeed "*kawaii*" in all aspects.

MORE FROM THIS AUTHOR

Below you'll find some of our other books that are popular on Amazon and Kindle as well. Alternatively, you can visit our author page on Amazon to see other work done by us.

3 Day Guide to Berlin: A 72-hour definitive guide on what to see, eat and enjoy in Berlin, Germany

3 Day Guide to Vienna: A 72-hour definitive guide on what to see, eat and enjoy in Vienna Austria

3 Day Guide to Santorini: A 72-hour definitive guide on what to see, eat and enjoy in Santorini Greece

3 Day Guide to Provence: A 72-hour definitive guide on what to see, eat and enjoy in Provence, France

3 Day Guide to Istanbul: A 72-hour definitive guide on what to see, eat and enjoy in Istanbul, Turkey

3 Day Guide to Budapest: A 72-hour Definitive Guide on What to See, Eat and Enjoy in Budapest, Hungary

3 Day Guide to Venice: A 72-hour Definitive Guide on What to See, Eat and Enjoy in Venice, Italy

3 Day Guide to Dublin: A 72-hour Definitive Guide on What to See, Eat and Enjoy in Dublin, Ireland

3 Day Guide to Singapore: A 72-hour Definitive Guide on What to See, Eat and Enjoy in Singapore, Singapore

3 Day Guide to Dubai: A 72-hour Definitive Guide on What to See, Eat and Enjoy in Dubai, UAE

CPSIA information can be obtained at www.ICGtesting.com
Printed in the USA
LVOW12s2038200515

439247LV00019B/200/P